TOSEL®

READING SERIES

READING

HIGH JUNIOR

1

CONTENTS

About TOSEL®

TOSEL (Test of Skills in the English Language) was developed to meet the demand for a more effective assessment of English as a foreign language for learners from specific cultural settings.

TOSEL evaluates and certifies the proficiency levels of English learners, from the age of 4 through adulthood, along with academic and job performance results.

Background

- Other English tests are ineffective in accurately measuring individual abilities
- Overuse of US-dominated testing systems in diverse cultural and educational contexts in the global English language learning market

Functions & Usage

- Assessment is categorized into 7 levels
- Used as a qualification for academic excellence for school admissions
- Used as a test to assess the English proficiency in the corporate and public sectors

Goals

- Create an effective tool for assessing and evaluating the English skills of English language learners
- Implement efficient and accessible testing systems and methods
- Provide constructive and developmental English education guidance

TOSEL® Strength

LEVELED ASSESSMENTS

An established English test system fit for seven different levels according to learners' cognitive development

ACCURATE DIAGNOSIS

A systematic and scientific diagnosis of learners' English proficiency

EXTENSIVE MATERIALS

Supplementary materials to help learners in an EFL environment to prepare for TOSEL and improve their proficiency

SUFFICIENT DATA

Content for each level developed by using data accumulated from more than 2,000,000 TOSEL test takers delegated at 15,000 schools and academies

CLASSIFIED AREAS OF INTELLIGENCE

Content designed to foster and expand the strengths of each student, categorized by the eight areas of intelligence

CONTINUITY

A complete course of English education ranging from kindergarten, elementary school, middle school, high schoool, and up to adults.

HIGH RELIABILITY

A high reliability level (Cronbach's alpha: .904 for elementary school students / .864 for university students) proven by several studies (Oxford University / Modern Language Journal)

SYSTEMATIC & EFFECTIVE ENGLISH EDUCATION

Accurate diagnosis and extensive materials which provide a step-by-step development in English learning, according to the quality of each learner's ability

TOSEL® Level Chart

Seven Separate Assessments

TOSEL divides the test into seven stages, by considering the test takers' cognitive levels, according to different ages. Unlike other assessments based on only one level, TOSEL includes separate assessments for preschool, elementary school, middle school, high school students, and for adults, which also includes both professionals and college students.

TOSEL's reporting system highlights the strengths and weaknesses of each test taker and suggests areas for further development.

COCOON

Suitable for children aged 4-6 (pre-schoolers)

The first step in the TOSEL system, the test is composed of colorful designs and interesting questions to interest young learners and to put them at ease.

Pre-STARTER

Suitable for children aged 7-8 (1st-2nd grades of elementary school)

Evaluates the ability to comprehend simple vocabulary, conversations, and sentences.

STARTER

Suitable for children aged 9-10 (3rd-4th grades of elementary school)

Evaluates the ability to comprehend short sentences and conversations related to everyday situations or topics.

BASIC

Suitable for children aged 11-12 (5th-6th grades of elementary school)

Evaluates the ability to communicate about personal information, daily activities, future plans, and past experiences in written and spoken language.

JUNIOR

Suitable for middle school students

Evaluates the ability to comprehend short paragraphs, practical texts, and speech covering general topics and to participate in simple daily conversations.

HIGH JUNIOR

Suitable for high school students

Evaluates the ability to use English fluently, accurately, and effectively on a wide range of social and academic subjects, as well as the ability to use sentences with a variety of complex structures.

ADVANCED

Suitable for university students and adults

Evaluates the ability to use practical English required for a job or work environment, as well as the ability to use and understand English at the university level.

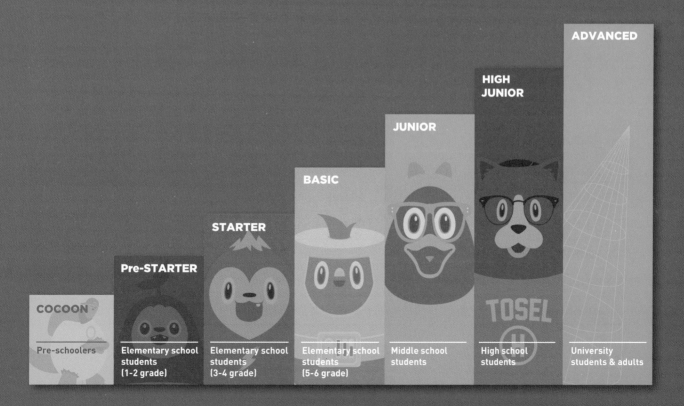

COCOON
Pre-schoolers

Pre-STARTER
Elementary school students (1-2 grade)

STARTER
Elementary school students (3-4 grade)

BASIC
Elementary school students (5-6 grade)

JUNIOR
Middle school students

HIGH JUNIOR
High school students

ADVANCED
University students & adults

Evaluation

Assessing the Four Skills

TOSEL evaluates the four language skills: reading, listening, speaking and writing, through indirect and direct assessment items.

This system of evaluation is part of a concerted effort to break away from materials geared solely toward grammar and reading-oriented education.

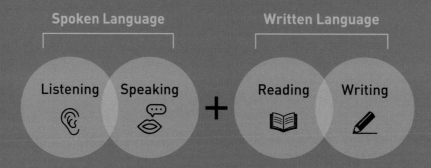

TOSEL Test Information

Level	Score	Grade	Section	
			Section I Listening & Speaking	Section II Reading & Writing
COCOON	100		15 Questions / 15 min	15 Questions / 15 min
Pre-STARTER	100		15 Questions / 15 min	20 Questions / 25 min
STARTER	100		20 Questions / 15 min	20 Questions / 25 min
BASIC	100	1-10	30 Questions / 20 min	30 Questions / 30 min
JUNIOR	100		30 Questions / 20 min	30 Questions / 30 min
HIGH JUNIOR	100		30 Questions / 25 min	35 Questions / 35 min
ADVANCED	990		70 Questions / 45 min	70 Questions / 55 min

Certificates

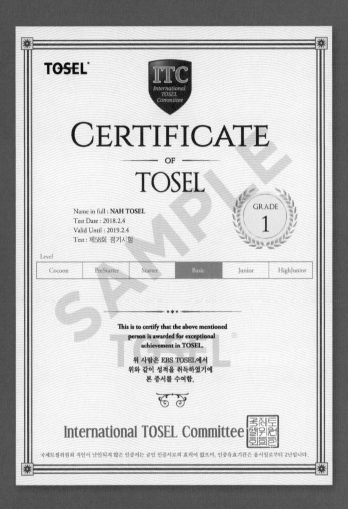

TOSEL Certificate

The International TOSEL Committee officially evaluates and certifies the level of English proficiency of English learners from the age of 4 to adults.

Certified by

Mar. 2010   Korea University
Dec. 2009   The Korean Society of Speech Science
Dec. 2009   The Korea Association of Foreign Language Education
Nov. 2009   The Applied Linguistics Association of Korea
Oct. 2009   The Pan Korea English Teachers Association

CHAPTER 1

Competitions 1

 Teacher's Book
p.44

UNIT 1

Toe Wrestling: UK

Have you ever heard of toe wrestling?
Do you think your toes are strong enough for wrestling?

Many have heard of or participated in arm wrestling or thumb wrestling, but what about toe wrestling? Every year hopeful world champions gather in the small English town of Fenny Bentley to see who is the best of the best at this little-known sport. But how did such a peculiar sport come to be?

Toe wrestling was started by four men who thought British people were not winning enough international championships. That is when they came up with a clever idea to create a new sport that not many people knew about. If the sport was unpopular, there would not be many contestants, and it would be easy for a British person to win.

In 1974, the group of men held the first "Toe Wrestling Championship." Indeed, a British person won that year and the next year, too! However, their plan backfired when someone visiting from Canada won in 1976. After that, the competition was not held for many years, but is now growing in popularity, with tourists and media outlets traveling to see the event every year.

New Words

contestant	**peculiar**
n a person in a competition	*adj* strange
come to be	**come up with**
v start to exist	*v* invent
clever	**backfire**
adj smart	*v* have the opposite effect than the one you want

Part A. Picture Description

1.

They decided to _____ to choose the new leader.

(A) take a vote
(B) arm wrestle
(C) draw names
(D) play rock-paper-scissors

2.

They thought Daveed's idea was quite _____.

(A) silly
(B) clever
(C) peculiar
(D) ridiculous

Part B. Sentence Completion

3.   We had never heard _____ the town before our trip, but we discovered we loved it!

(A) in
(B) of
(C) at
(D) to

4.   She hurt her thumb when the door closed. _____ is when she decided to be more careful.

(A) So
(B) And
(C) That
(D) There

Got Strong Toes?
Be a Toe Wrestler!

You need:

- strong feet
- no signs of fungus or injury on your toes (You will be examined by a podiatrist immediately prior to the competition.)
- a fighter's spirit

See if you can break reigning champion
Alan "Nasty" Nash 14-year streak
at the Bentley Brook Inn. Friday, June 14, 7 PM

Check out our Bookface webpage here
for more information!

5. According to the notice, what must toe wrestlers do?

   (A) get their feet tested by a foot doctor
   (B) bring fungus medication for their feet
   (C) measure their feet against their competitors'
   (D) bring in a hospital note explaining past foot injuries

6. Why is the champion's nickname most likely "Nasty"?

   (A) He competes in Nashville.
   (B) He has cheated for fourteen years.
   (C) He suffers from chronic toe fungus.
   (D) He is tough and his last name is Nash.

Part D. General Reading Comprehension

Many have heard of or participated in arm wrestling or thumb wrestling, but what about toe wrestling? Every year hopeful world champions gather in the small English town of Fenny Bentley to see who is the best of the best at this little-known sport. But how did such a peculiar sport come to be?

Toe wrestling was started by four men who thought British people were not winning enough international championships. That is when they came up with a clever idea to create a new sport that not many people knew about. If the sport was unpopular, there would not be many contestants, and it would be easy for a British person to win.

In 1974, the group of men held the first "Toe Wrestling Championship." Indeed, a British person won that year, and the next year, too! However, <u>their plan</u> backfired when someone visiting from Canada won in 1976. After that, the competition was not held for many years, but is now growing in popularity, with tourists and media outlets traveling to see the event every year.

7. What is the passage mainly about?

    (A) the rules of toe wrestling
    (B) reasons why toe wrestling failed
    (C) how toe wrestling was developed
    (D) where toe wrestling can be watched

8. Which sport is NOT listed?

    (A) toe wrestling
    (B) ear wrestling
    (C) arm wrestling
    (D) thumb wrestling

9. What is mentioned about the Toe Wrestling Championship?

    (A) It takes place in a small town.
    (B) It often involves player injuries.
    (C) Competitors play three rounds.
    (D) Competitors must remove their shoes.

10. What does the underlined "their plan" refer to?

    (A) the judges' idea to change the rules
    (B) the winners' decision to share the prize
    (C) the organizers' plan for a British person to win
    (D) the competitors' strategy to change the contest rules

Listening Practice

 Listen and write.

  MP3 HJ1-1

Toe Wrestling: UK

Many have heard of or participated in arm wrestling or thumb wrestling, but what about toe wrestling? Every year hopeful world champions gather in the small English town of Fenny Bentley to see who is the best of the best at this little-known sport. But how did such a ^1 _____ sport ^2 _____ ?

Toe wrestling was started by four men who thought British people were not winning enough international championships. That is when they ^3 _____ a ^4 _____ idea to create a new sport that not many people knew about. If the sport was unpopular, there would not be many ^5 _____ , and it would be easy for a British person to win. In 1974, the group of men held the first "Toe Wrestling Championship." Indeed, a British person won that year, and the next year, too! However, their plan ^6 _____ when someone visiting from Canada won in 1976. After that, the competition was not held for many years, but is now growing in popularity, with tourists and media outlets traveling to see the event every year.

Word Bank

come to be	came up with	peculiar
backfired	contestants	cameupwith
clever	peckuliar	cliver
came to be	contestents	beckfired

 Listen. Pause. Say each sentence.

  MP3 HJ1-1G

Writing Practice

 Write the words.

1 _____

[n] a person in a competition

2 _____

[adj] strange

3 _____

[v] start to exist

4 _____

[v] invent

5 _____

[adj] smart

6 _____

[v] have the opposite effect than the one you want

 Write the words in each blank.

Summary

The _____ "Toe Wrestling Championship" was held in 1974. It _____ for many years; however, the _____ sport is now becoming _____ with tourists and media outlets traveling to see the event.

Word Puzzle

 Complete the word puzzle.

Across

4 have the opposite effect than the one you want

6 strange

Down

1 invent

2 start to exist

3 a person in a competition

5 smart

UNIT 2

 Teacher's Book p.49

Chessboxing

Chess and boxing are different but can go together.
Ice cream and spicy peppers are also different but can go together.
Name other things that seem different but that go together.

Few would think that the physical sport of boxing and the mental sport of chess have much in common, but the two have been combined into a worldwide sporting event since 2003. The first chessboxing match was organized by Iepe Rubingh, a Dutch performance artist. With alternating 3-minute rounds of chess and boxing, a win in any of the rounds would win the entire match. Rubingh wanted to break down the barriers humans make by putting things into categories, so he combined two very different competitions. Viewers of the art performance loved the newly-invented sport, and fandoms quickly grew in several countries, including Great Britain, Russia, India, and Germany.

In order to enter the World Chessboxing Championships, all participants must have a certified level of skill in both chess and boxing. This prevents the athletes from only focusing on one of the two sports. Each match consists of 13 rounds, 7 rounds of chess with 6 rounds of boxing in between. With only a 60-second resting time between each round, a full match of chessboxing is an exhausting 51 minutes of fast-paced back-and-forth battle of both brains and muscles.

New Words

mental adj of the mind	**Dutch** adj from the Netherlands
alternating adj first A, then B, then A, then B, etc..	**category** n group
certified adj officially proven	**exhausting** adj extremely tiring

Part A. Picture Description

10 minutes

1.

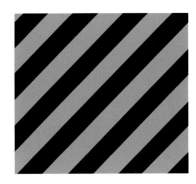

The pattern has _____ yellow and black lines.

(A) alternating
(B) intersecting
(C) criss-crossing
(D) perpendicular

2.

The journey was _____.

(A) easy
(B) effortless
(C) expensive
(D) exhausting

Part B. Sentence Completion

3. Turning off your TV can prevent you _____ staying up too late.

(A) on
(B) for
(C) from
(D) over

4. Diana's birthday party is _____ by her parents and friends.

(A) organize
(B) organizes
(C) organized
(D) organizing

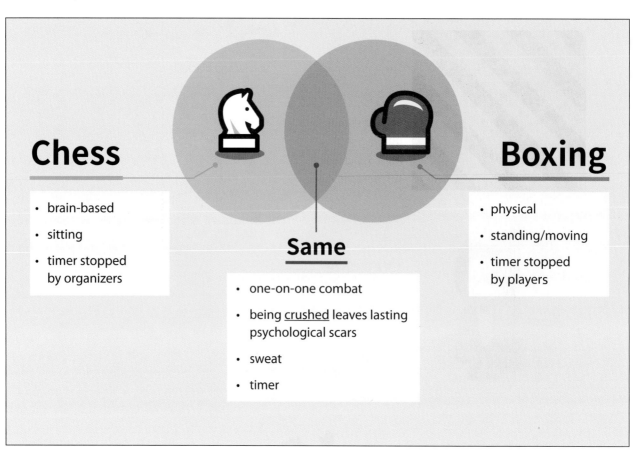

5. Which is mentioned about the sports?

   (A) what players wear
   (B) how long matches last
   (C) the building players use
   (D) the mental effects on players

6. The underlined "crushed" is most similar in meaning to:

   (A) stuck
   (B) stopped
   (C) defeated
   (D) disappointed

Part D. General Reading Comprehension

Few would think that the physical sport of boxing and the mental sport of chess have much in common, but the two have been combined into a worldwide sporting event since 2003. The first chessboxing match was organized by Iepe Rubingh, a Dutch performance artist. With alternating 3-minute rounds of chess and boxing, a win in any of the rounds would win the entire match. Rubingh wanted to break down the barriers humans make by putting things into categories, so he combined two very different competitions. Viewers of the art performance loved the newly-invented sport, and fandoms quickly grew in several countries, including Great Britain, Russia, India, and Germany.

In order to enter the World Chessboxing Championships, all participants must have a certified level of skill in both chess and boxing. This prevents the athletes from only focusing on one of the two sports. Each match consists of 13 rounds, 7 rounds of chess with 6 rounds of boxing in between. With only a 60-second resting time between each round, a full match of chessboxing is an exhausting 51 minutes of fast-paced back-and-forth battle of both brains and muscles.

7. What would be the best title for this passage?

(A) An Unusual Match
(B) How to Defend Yourself
(C) New Strategies for Old Games
(D) All You Wanted to Know About Sports

8. What country was the creator of Chessboxing from?

(A) Russia
(B) Germany
(C) Great Britain
(D) the Netherlands

9. How many minutes long is each round of boxing?

(A) 1
(B) 3
(C) 6
(D) 7

10. According to the passage, which of the following statements is true?

(A) A chessboxing match always starts with boxing.
(B) Matches can end before the final round is played.
(C) Chessboxing has been an official sport for five decades.
(D) Contestants only need a high rank in either chess or boxing.

 Listen and write.

  MP3 HJ1-2

Chessboxing

Few would think that the physical sport of boxing and the ¹ _____ sport of chess have much in common, but the two have been combined into a worldwide sporting event since 2003. The first chessboxing match was organized by Iepe Rubingh, a ² _____ performance artist. With ³ _____ 3-minute rounds of chess and boxing, a win in any of the rounds would win the entire match. Rubingh wanted to break down the barriers humans make by putting things into ⁴ _____ , so he combined two very different competitions. Viewers of the art performance loved the newly-invented sport, and fandoms quickly grew in several countries, including Great Britain, Russia, India, and Germany.

In order to enter the World Chessboxing Championships, all participants must have a ⁵ _____ level of skill in both chess and boxing. This prevents the athletes from only focusing on one of the two sports. Each match consists of 13 rounds, 7 rounds of chess with 6 rounds of boxing in between. With only a 60-second resting time between each round, a full match of chessboxing is an ⁶ _____ 51 minutes of fast-paced back-and-forth battle of both brains and muscles.

Word Bank

mental	alternating	Dutch
certified	category	certify
exhausting	metal	categories
exausting	dutch	alterneting

 Listen. Pause. Say each sentence.

  MP3 HJ1-2G

Writing Practice

 Write the words.

1 _____ *adj* of the mind	2 _____ *adj* from the Netherlands
3 _____ *adj* first A, then B, then A, then B, etc..	4 _____ *n* group
5 _____ *adj* officially proven	6 _____ *adj* extremely tiring

 Write the words in each blank.

Summary

Two very different competitions, the physical sport of boxing and the _____ sport of chess have been _____ into the World Chessboxing Championships. To enter this _____ sporting event, all participants must have a _____ level of skill in both chess and boxing.

Word Puzzle

 Complete the word puzzle.

Across

2 from the Netherlands

6 first A, then B, then A, then B, etc..

Down

1 extremely tiring

3 officially proven

4 of the mind

5 group

Teacher's Book
p.54

UNIT 3

The World Memory Championships

Imagine that you have a deck of cards.
Shuffle the cards. Then memorize the order of the cards.
How many cards can you remember?

Most people can remember things like phone numbers and faces of classmates. However, the majority are not used to memorizing the order of an entire deck of playing cards in a matter of minutes — a skill that competitors at the World Memory Championships have mastered. The competition challenges contestants in a number of categories, including ones related to names, faces, numbers, and even random words. In 2019, the winner of the competition's children's category memorized the order of over seven decks of shuffled cards within an hour, 1,155 numbers within half an hour, and 87 names and faces within a quarter of an hour.

The majority of the contestants in the competition use the ancient Roman technique of "memory palaces" to keep track of long lists of information. This technique involves linking items of information to a place that the memorizer knows well. Using methods such as memory palaces and preparing with countless hours of practice, contestants at the World Memory Championships remind us that the ability to learn things by heart is not just a born gift, but rather a skill that can be coached and built up over time.

New Words

memorize *v* remember on purpose	**in a matter of minutes** *adv* in just a few minutes
master *v* get really good at	**shuffled** *adj* arranged in a random order
keep track of *v* be aware of and remember	**countless** *adj* many

Part A. Picture Description

1.

Can you _____ this deck for us?

(A) beat
(B) deal
(C) move
(D) shuffle

2.

Keiko is _____ the money she has earned.

(A) making fun of
(B) standing up for
(C) keeping track of
(D) getting away from

Part B. Sentence Completion

3. My mom had to get used to _____ on the left-hand side of the road in Japan.

(A) drive
(B) driver
(C) driving
(D) be drive

4. For this test, you need to remember a lot of random _____.

(A) information
(B) informations
(C) these information
(D) these informations

"Three Strikes You're Out"

In this challenge, eight mental athletes (MAs) get 20 minutes to hear facts about seven different random people. The information includes the person's name, birthday (including day, month, and year), current town of residence, email address, pet type and name, two hobbies, two favorite foods, and favorite vehicle make and model. Each MA will see the information in writing and hear it spoken.

After 20 minutes, the MAs will be selected at random to recall the information orally. The seven people will be brought back to appear before the MAs, but in a different order than their original appearance. The time limit to answer about each person is only 15 seconds. All information must be correct and complete. After three incorrect or incomplete answers, the MA will be eliminated.

5. Which of the following bits of information are the MAs NOT asked to memorize about each person?

(A) preferred food
(B) domestic animal
(C) free time activity
(D) languages spoken

6. Which of the following is true about the challenge?

(A) MAs are given 15 seconds to memorize.
(B) MAs leave after three incorrect answers.
(C) MAs appear in a new order to recite answers.
(D) MAs have 20 minutes to talk to random people.

Part D. General Reading Comprehension

Most people can remember things like phone numbers and faces of classmates. However, the majority are not used to memorizing the order of an entire deck of playing cards in a matter of minutes — a skill that competitors at the World Memory Championships have mastered. The competition challenges contestants in a number of categories, including ones related to names, faces, numbers, and even random words. In 2019, the winner of the competition's children's category memorized the order of over seven decks of shuffled cards within an hour, 1,155 numbers within half an hour, and 87 names and faces within a quarter of an hour.

The majority of the contestants in the competition use the ancient Roman technique of "memory palaces" to keep track of long lists of information. This technique involves linking items of information to a place that the memorizer knows well. Using methods such as memory palaces and preparing with countless hours of practice, contestants at the World Memory Championships remind us that the ability to learn things by heart is not just a born gift, but rather a skill that can be coached and built up over time.

7. Which World Memory Championship event category is NOT mentioned in the passage?

(A) numbers
(B) historic dates
(C) random words
(D) names and faces

8. What did one 2019 champion do?

(A) match 30 pictures of people to a description
(B) shuffle seven decks of cards in the same order
(C) take one hour to learn over 87 names and faces
(D) memorize over one thousand numbers in half an hour

9. What is the main idea of the second paragraph?

(A) Formal memorization techniques began in Rome.
(B) Most contestants dislike practicing for competitions.
(C) Contestants practice to become memorization champions.
(D) Memorizing is generally easier for people with natural ability.

10. According to the passage, how does a memory palace work?

(A) Memorizers think about royal names.
(B) Memorizers connect data to song lyrics.
(C) Memorizers link information to a place they know.
(D) Memorizers put up a mental barrier against unwanted thoughts.

 Listen and write.

  MP3 HJ1-3

The World Memory Championships

Most people can remember things like phone numbers and faces of classmates. However, the majority are not used to memorizing the order of an entire deck of playing cards in a ¹ _____ of minutes — a skill that competitors at the World Memory Championships have ² _____. The competition challenges contestants in a number of categories, including ones related to names, faces, numbers, and even random words.

In 2019, the winner of the competition's children's category ³ _____ the order of over seven decks of ⁴ _____ cards within an hour, 1,155 numbers within half an hour, and 87 names and faces within a quarter of an hour.

The majority of the contestants in the competition use the ancient Roman technique of "memory palaces" to ⁵ _____ long lists of information. This technique involves linking items of information to a place that the memorizer knows well. Using methods such as memory palaces and preparing with ⁶ _____ hours of practice, contestants at the World Memory Championships remind us that the ability to learn things by heart is not just a born gift, but rather a skill that can be coached and built up over time.

Word Bank

shuffle	matter	masters
contless	shuffled	memoried
memorized	mastered	manner
keeptrackof	countless	keep track of

 Listen. Pause. Say each sentence.

  MP3 HJ1-3G

Writing Practice

 Write the words.

1 _____	2 _____
v remember on purpose	*adv* in just a few minutes
3 _____	4 _____
v get really good at	*adj* arranged in a random order
5 _____	6 _____
v be aware of and remember	*adj* many

 Write the words in each blank.

Summary

_____ at the World Memory Championships have _____ the art of

_____. Most of the contestants in the competition use special methods to

_____ long lists of information.

Word Puzzle

 Complete the word puzzle.

Across

2 in just a few minutes

4 remember on purpose

5 arranged in a random order

Down

1 be aware of and remember

3 many

4 get really good at

UNIT 4

The O Henry Pun-Off

Teacher's Book p.59

Tell a joke based on word play.
It can be in English or in your own language.

Some people love them, and some people hate them, but almost everyone seems to have a strong opinion about puns. Often called "dad jokes" by people who do not find them funny, puns are usually short statements that play with the meanings (or sounds) of words to produce humor. Fans of such jokes gather every year in Austin, Texas to participate in the O. Henry Pun-Off and crown the person with the best puns.

The competition is named after the author O. Henry (born "William Sydney Porter," 1862-1910), who was known for writing short stories with surprising endings and clever word play. The founders of the Pun-Off wanted to continue this tradition and began the competition in 1978. As time went on, the number of contestants grew, and the rules became more and more complicated. Now, a panel of six judges gives participants a score from 1 to 10. The top and bottom scores are removed, and the contestant with the highest score out of 40 is named "Punniest of Show" that year.

New Words

pun	**joke**
n a humorous statement that plays with words	*n* a humorous statement
crown X	**word play**
v make X the king or queen	*n* jokes with words
complicated	**judge**
adj not simple	*n* a person who chooses a winner

10 minutes

1.

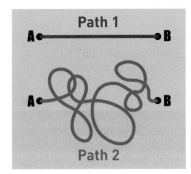

Path 2 is relatively _____.

(A) calm
(B) simple
(C) straight
(D) complicated

2.

One of the _____ has a mustache.

(A) judges
(B) lawyers
(C) accused
(D) defendants

Part B. Sentence Completion

3. The beginning of the movie was very predictable, but the ending was _____.

(A) surprise
(B) surprised
(C) surprising
(D) the surprised

4. This city is getting _____ crowded each year.

(A) more to more
(B) most or more
(C) more and most
(D) more and more

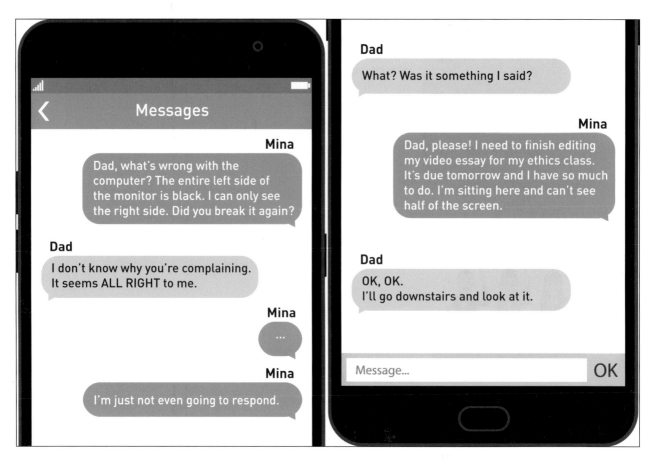

5. What is Mina's problem?

   (A) Her computer has frozen.
   (B) One half of her monitor is dark.
   (C) Her monitor has become blurry.
   (D) One side of her keyboard has failed.

6. What does Mina most likely mean when she says, "I'm just not even going to respond"?

   (A) She will not mention her dad's pun.
   (B) She has decided not to do her homework.
   (C) She will not help her father with a video essay.
   (D) She does not understand her computer problem.

Part D. General Reading Comprehension

Some people love them, and some people hate them, but almost everyone seems to have a strong opinion about puns. Often called "dad jokes" by people who do not find them funny, puns are usually short statements that play with the meanings (or sounds) of words to produce humor. Fans of such jokes gather every year in Austin, Texas to participate in the O. Henry Pun-Off and crown the person with the best puns.

The competition is named after the author O. Henry (born "William Sydney Porter," 1862-1910), who was known for writing short stories with surprising endings and clever word play. The founders of the Pun-Off wanted to continue this tradition and began the competition in 1978. As time went on, the number of contestants grew, and the rules became more and more complicated. Now, a panel of six judges gives participants a score from 1 to 10. The top and bottom scores are removed, and the contestant with the highest score out of 40 is named "Punniest of Show" that year.

7. What is the main topic of this passage?

(A) a spelling bee
(B) a clever author
(C) a joke competition
(D) a storytelling tournament

8. According to the passage, which of these best describes "puns"?

(A) based on word sounds
(B) started in Austin, Texas
(C) enjoyed by most people
(D) made famous by O. Henry

9. When did the O. Henry Pun-Off begin?

(A) 1862
(B) 1910
(C) 1978
(D) 2003

10. How many judges are in the panel at the O. Henry Pun-Off?

(A) 1
(B) 4
(C) 6
(D) 10

Listening Practice

 Listen and write.

The O Henry Pun-Off

Some people love them, and some people hate them, but almost everyone seems to have a strong opinion about ¹_____. Often called "dad jokes" by people who do not find them funny, puns are usually short statements that play with the meanings (or sounds) of words to produce humor. Fans of such ²_____ gather every year in Austin, Texas to participate in the O. Henry Pun-Off and ³_____ the person with the best puns. The competition is named after the author O. Henry (born "William Sydney Porter," 1862-1910), who was known for writing short stories with surprising endings and clever ⁴_____. The founders of the Pun-Off wanted to continue this tradition and began the competition in 1978. As time went on, the number of contestants grew, and the rules became more and more ⁵_____. Now, a panel of six ⁶_____ gives participants a score from 1 to 10. The top and bottom scores are removed, and the contestant with the highest score out of 40 is named "Punniest of Show" that year.

Word Bank

judgers	word play	crown
complicated	judges	puns
jokes	complicate	word pray
joke	funs	crowne

 Listen. Pause. Say each sentence.

Writing Practice

 Write the words.

1 _____ *n* a humorous statement that plays with words	2 _____ *n* a humorous statement
3 _____ X *v* make X the king or queen	4 _____ *n* jokes with words
5 _____ *adj* not simple	6 _____ *n* a person who chooses a winner

 Write the words in each blank.

Summary

Puns are short _____ that play with the meanings or sounds of words to produce _____. Every year, the O. Henry Pun-Off, named after the famously _____ author, is held to _____ the person with the best puns.

Word Puzzle

 Complete the word puzzle.

Across

2 jokes with words

5 make X the king or queen

6 a person who chooses a winner

Down

1 not simple

3 a humorous statement that plays with words

4 a humorous statement

AMAZING STORIES

Henry Molaison: Patient H.M.

Teacher's Book
p.64

Henry Molaison was a young American who had long suffered from terrible seizures. In 1953, when he was 27 years old, a team of doctors performed surgery on his brain in an effort to help stop the seizures. After the surgery, Molaison did have fewer seizures. But he also had something else: an inability to store any new memories. He could only remember memories created before the age of sixteen. After the surgery, he would forget new information within 30 seconds. Molaison, known only as Patient H.M., would go on to become the most famous patient in the new field of brain science.

Brain scientists learned many new things from Molaison's case. One of the most important discoveries was that memories are not "stored" by the whole brain; rather, certain parts of the brain control certain types of memories. They also discovered the difference between unconscious and conscious memory. For example, Molaison could still learn new physical skills, like how to use a walking tool when he hurt his ankle.

However, the brain and the mind still remain scientific mysteries. What is more, research into Molaison's case has revealed other mysteries. When Molaison died in 2008, a cut on his brain was discovered that had been little studied before. In addition, a lead researcher was quoted in an interview as saying that she had destroyed original data from experiments conducted on Molaison. However, because Molaison's brain was cut into over 2,000 pieces for scientific study, the mysteries surrounding the case of Patient H.M. may remain secrets forever.

CHAPTER 2

Competitions 2

UNIT 5

 Teacher's Book p.65

The Air Guitar Championships

Pretend you are playing a musical instrument.
Your friend guesses:
1) What instrument is it?
2) What song are you playing?

At a yearly competition in Oulu, Finland, contestants do not need to be able to make a single sound on a real instrument. They just need to be the best at playing a guitar that does not exist. Air guitar involves a performer pretending to play an invisible electric or acoustic guitar. And at the Air Guitar World Championships in Oulu, only the best get to show their skills at dancing, making faces, and miming the act of playing the guitar.

The competition includes two rounds. In the first round, competitors perform a 60-second song they prepare in advance. In the second round, competitors perform a 60-second song chosen by the contest organizers. They hear the song right before they perform it. The performances are given a maximum score of 6.0 points for each round; both rounds count for the total.

The Air Guitar World Championships started out as a sideshow during a music video festival. However, it has now taken on a bigger meaning. According to the organization's official website, the championships serve to "promote world peace." As the organizers remind us, we should all "make air, not war."

New Words

pretend	invisible
v act as if	adj not shown to the eye

acoustic	mime
adj not electric	v physically pretend

take on	promote
v begin to have	v actively support

Part A. Picture Description

1.

He _____ leaning on chair.

(A) fell
(B) began
(C) mimed
(D) tripped

2.

My guitar is _____.

(A) electric
(B) missing
(C) acoustic
(D) invisible

Part B. Sentence Completion

3. For this contest, you need to _____ dance well.

(A) can
(B) able to
(C) be able to
(D) can be able to

4. We started the event just for fun, but it has now _____ on an important meaning.

(A) take
(B) took
(C) taken
(D) been taken

Registration Form for All-ages Winfield Air Band/ Lip Sync Contest

Saturday, March 14, 2020
7:30 PM (doors open at 6:30)   Form and fees must be submitted between February 21 and March 7, 2020

Name(s): [   ]

Contact person: [   ]   Email of contact person: [   ]

Phone #: [   ]   Category: ☐ Kids   ☐ Adults

Name of your song: [   ]   **Time of song** (maximum 4 minutes long): [   ]

Registration fee: [   ] band members × $5.00 = [   ]

Family tickets needed: [   ] adults × $8.00 = [   ]

[   ] youth (under 16) × $5.00 = [   ]

Do you want a DVD recording of the show?: [   ] × $10.00 each = [   ]   **Total $** [   ]

Note:
- Songs may not contain any swearing. It is an all-ages show. The organizers reserve the right to refuse any song deemed not appropriate.
- All performers must be present at a technical rehearsal on Saturday, March 7, 2020 between 1:30 PM and 5:00 PM at the Century Memorial hall. You will be notified of the exact schedule by February 26.

---

5. The band "Krystal" has four members. Two want a DVD, and each member is bringing one youth and one adult guest. How much is the total?

    (A) 20
    (B) 56
    (C) 92
    (D) 112

6. Which is most likely a reason why organizers would refuse an entrant?

    (A) They are under the required age.
    (B) Their song is under four minutes.
    (C) Their song contains an obscene word.
    (D) They submitted their form on March 6th.

Part D. General Reading Comprehension

At a yearly competition in Oulu, Finland, contestants do not need to be able to make a single sound on a real instrument. They just need to be the best at playing a guitar that does not exist. Air guitar involves a performer pretending to play an invisible electric or acoustic guitar. And at the Air Guitar World Championships in Oulu, only the best get to show their skills at dancing, making faces, and miming the act of playing the guitar.

The competition includes two rounds. In the first round, competitors perform a 60-second song they prepare in advance. In the second round, competitors perform a 60-second song chosen by the contest organizers. They hear the song right before they perform it. The performances are given a maximum score of 6.0 points for each round; both rounds count for the total.

The Air Guitar World Championships started out as a sideshow during a music video festival. However, it has now taken on a bigger meaning. According to the organization's official website, the championships serve to "promote world peace." As the organizers remind us, we should all "make air, not war."

7. What would be the best title of the passage?

   (A) How Oulu Invented the Guitar
   (B) Playing Imaginary Guitars in Oulu
   (C) Oulu: A Hub for Musicians from Finland
   (D) Why Finland's Oulu Sells the Most Guitars

8. Which is NOT listed as a skill performed in the competition?

   (A) mime
   (B) dance
   (C) face-making
   (D) body-painting

9. What is the maximum score a competitor could get in the competition?

   (A) 6
   (B) 10
   (C) 12
   (D) 24

10. Which quote would a competition organizer most likely write?

   (A) "This show features the world's best singers."
   (B) "This performance festival is mainly for military music."
   (C) "This competition promotes our vision of peace on Earth."
   (D) "This contest symbolizes revenge for our cancelled music video."

 Listen and write.

  MP3 HJ1-5

The Air Guitar Championships

At a yearly competition in Oulu, Finland, contestants do not need to be able to make a single sound on a real instrument. They just need to be the best at playing a guitar that does not exist.

Air guitar involves a performer ¹ _____ to play an ² _____ electric or ³ _____ guitar. And at the Air Guitar World Championships in Oulu, only the best get to show their skills at dancing, making faces, and ⁴ _____ the act of playing the guitar.

The competition includes two rounds. In the first round, competitors perform a 60-second song they prepare in advance. In the second round, competitors perform a 60-second song chosen by the contest organizers. They hear the song right before they perform it. The performances are given a maximum score of 6.0 points for each round; both rounds count for the total.

The Air Guitar World Championships started out as a sideshow during a music video festival. However, it has now ⁵ _____ a bigger meaning. According to the organization's official website, the championships serve to " ⁶ _____ world peace." As the organizers remind us, we should all "make air, not war."

Word Bank

invisible	acoustic	taking on
visible	pritending	miming
taken on	mimed	promote
pretending	acoostic	premote

 Listen. Pause. Say each sentence.

  MP3 HJ1-5G

Writing Practice

 Write the words.

1 _____

v act as if

2 _____

adj not shown to the eye

3 _____

adj not electric

4 _____

v physically pretend

5 _____

v begin to have

6 _____

v actively support

 Write the words in each blank.

Summary

The Air Guitar World Championships is an _____ competition in Finland which crowns a person with the best air guitar _____. Although this competition started as a _____ of a festival, now it has a bigger meaning to "_____ world peace."

Word Puzzle

 Complete the word puzzle.

Across

4 act as if

5 physically pretend

Down

1 not shown to the eye

2 begin to have

3 not electric

4 actively support

UNIT 6

Teacher's Book p.70

Mistakes at the Academy Awards

Have you ever planned a big event?
If so, did anything go wrong? If not, what might go wrong?

Televised award shows are big events that require a lot of careful planning. Nonetheless, because they happen live, many things can go wrong. Nowhere is this more apparent than at the Academy Awards in Hollywood, California.

The ceremony infamously had a horrible moment in 2014. A presenter was introducing the singer who would perform "Let It Go" from the movie *Frozen*. "Ladies and gentlemen... Adela Dazeem!" said the presenter. The singer's actual name was Idina Menzel.

A worse mistake happened at the 2017 ceremony. During the category for Best Picture, the biggest award of the night, the presenter was given the wrong card. He ended up announcing *La La Land* as the best movie instead of the real winner, *Moonlight*. Sadly, the makers of *La La Land* were already on stage giving an acceptance speech when the mistake was discovered.

However, perhaps the most embarrassing occurrence was at the 46th Academy Awards in 1974. Just as the presenters were preparing to announce a winner, a man ran naked across the stage. As these and other events demonstrate, even carefully planned events like the Academy Awards can have major issues.

New Words

televised *adj* on TV	**nonetheless** *adv* nevertheless
apparent *adj* obvious	**infamously** *adv* famously in a bad way
acceptance speech *n* the words a winner says when receiving a prize	**naked** *adj* without any clothes on

Part A. Picture Description

1.

The game was _____.

(A) televised
(B) telephoned
(C) telescoped
(D) telegrammed

2.

He thanked his parents in his _____.

(A) lengthy letter
(B) text message
(C) acceptance speech
(D) video conference call

Part B. Sentence Completion

3. I love winter, and nowhere _____ more beautiful than in my hometown in Russia.

(A) is it
(B) it is
(C) has there
(D) there has

4. We ended up _____ the party early because Martin felt sick.

(A) leave
(B) leaving
(C) to leave
(D) had to leave

UNIT 6 Mistakes at the Academy Awards

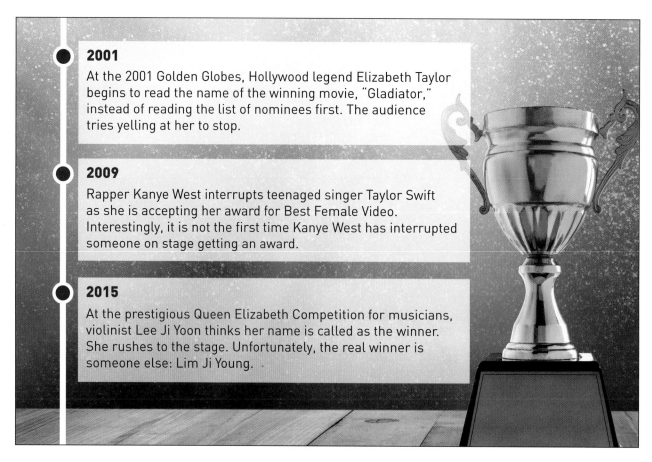

2001

At the 2001 Golden Globes, Hollywood legend Elizabeth Taylor begins to read the name of the winning movie, "Gladiator," instead of reading the list of nominees first. The audience tries yelling at her to stop.

2009

Rapper Kanye West interrupts teenaged singer Taylor Swift as she is accepting her award for Best Female Video. Interestingly, it is not the first time Kanye West has interrupted someone on stage getting an award.

2015

At the prestigious Queen Elizabeth Competition for musicians, violinist Lee Ji Yoon thinks her name is called as the winner. She rushes to the stage. Unfortunately, the real winner is someone else: Lim Ji Young.

5. When did someone forget to read the list of nominees?

(A) 2001

(B) 2009

(C) 2015

(D) both 2009 and 2015

6. What happened to a violinist?

(A) She fell off a stage.

(B) She won Best Female Video.

(C) She misheard the winner's name.

(D) She yelled at an audience member.

Part D. General Reading Comprehension

Televised award shows are big events that require a lot of careful planning. Nonetheless, because they happen live, many things can go wrong. Nowhere is this more apparent than at the Academy Awards in Hollywood, California.

The ceremony infamously had a horrible moment in 2014. A presenter was introducing the singer who would perform "Let It Go" from the movie *Frozen*. "Ladies and gentlemen... Adela Dazeem!" said the presenter. The singer's actual name was Idina Menzel.

A worse mistake happened at the 2017 ceremony. During the category for Best Picture, the biggest award of the night, the presenter was given the wrong card. He ended up announcing *La La Land* as the best movie instead of the real winner, *Moonlight*. Sadly, the makers of *La La Land* were already on stage giving an acceptance speech when the mistake was discovered.

However, perhaps the most embarrassing occurrence was at the 46th Academy Awards in 1974. Just as the presenters were preparing to announce a winner, a man ran naked across the stage. As these and other events demonstrate, even carefully planned events like the Academy Awards can have major issues.

7. What is the passage mainly about?

(A) problems at the Academy Awards
(B) the least popular films in Hollywood
(C) protests against the Academy Awards
(D) viewing numbers of Hollywood ceremonies

8. According to the passage, what problem happened in 2014?

(A) An actor fell off the stage.
(B) A singer forgot some lyrics.
(C) An animation film clip did not play.
(D) A presenter mispronounced a name.

9. According to the passage, what went wrong in 2017?

(A) A presenter dropped his card.
(B) A presenter could not stop laughing.
(C) The wrong Best Picture winner was announced.
(D) The winners of Best Picture left the theater early.

10. According to the passage, in which year(s) did a nude person disrupt the ceremony?

(A) 1974
(B) 2017
(C) 1974 and 2014
(D) 2014 and 2017

Listening Practice

 Listen and write.

  MP3 HJ1-6

Mistakes at the Academy Awards

1 _____ award shows are big events that require a lot of careful planning.
2 _____, because they happen live, many things can go wrong. Nowhere is this more 3 _____ than at the Academy Awards in Hollywood, California.

The ceremony 4 _____ had a horrible moment in 2014. A presenter was introducing the singer who would perform "Let It Go" from the movie *Frozen*. "Ladies and gentlemen... Adela Dazeem!" said the presenter. The singer's actual name was Idina Menzel. A worse mistake happened at the 2017 ceremony. During the category for Best Picture, the biggest award of the night, the presenter was given the wrong card. He ended up announcing *La La Land* as the best movie instead of the real winner, *Moonlight*. Sadly, the makers of *La La Land* were already on stage giving an 5 _____ speech when the mistake was discovered.

However, perhaps the most embarrassing occurrence was at the 46th Academy Awards in 1974.

Just as the presenters were preparing to announce a winner, a man ran 6 _____ across the stage. As these and other events demonstrate, even carefully planned events like the Academy Awards can have major issues.

Word Bank

acceptants	televised	apperent
nakid	infamously	naked
acceptance	enfamously	apparent
Nonetheless	Nontheless	Televised

 Listen. Pause. Say each sentence.

  MP3 HJ1-6G

Writing Practice

 Write the words.

1 _____

adj on TV

2 _____

adv nevertheless

3 _____

adj obvious

4 _____

adv famously in a bad way

5 _____

n the words a winner says when receiving a prize

6 _____

adj without any clothes on

 Write the words in each blank.

Summary

The Academy Awards in Hollywood, California has had several problems over the years. _____, a presenter _____ the name of a singer, the wrong Best Picture winner was _____, and a _____ man ran across the stage.

Word Puzzle

 Complete the word puzzle.

Across

2 nevertheless

5 on TV

6 without any clothes on

Down

1 famously in a bad way

3 the words a winner says when receiving a prize

4 obvious

UNIT 7

Extreme Ironing

Teacher's Book p.76

Have you ever used an iron? What did you iron?

UNIT 7 Extreme Ironing

Ironing a shirt is a challenge for many people. In the competitive sport of extreme ironing, however, that challenge is taken to a different level as competitors press clothing in extreme places and conditions.

There are different rules for the diverse extreme ironing competitions held around the world, but the general rules are similar. Ironers must have a full-sized ironing board, a real iron, and a piece of clothing larger than a face towel. Very importantly, the ironers need to be video-recorded so that others can see them compete.

Spectators cannot typically view the competitors in action because the ironing needs to take place in extreme conditions. In the past, contestants have ironed in trees, on rooftops, on steep cliffs, on mountaintops, on ropes suspended between rocks, in icy glacier water, and in dry deserts. Extreme ironing has even happened on the ocean floor by ironers who were divers.

Extreme ironers are advised to take safety precautions. However, like all extreme sports, this kind of ironing comes with some risks. For adventurous athletes who also want to complete household chores, extreme ironing might be just the right kind of competition.

New Words

iron	**press**
v take wrinkles out of clothes	*v* iron
glacier	**suspended**
n a big mass of ice	*adj* hanging
precaution	**chore**
n a way to avoid risk	*n* a task

Part A. Picture Description

1.

I saw bears _____ during my recent trip.

(A) being fed
(B) on a glacier
(C) in zoo cages
(D) in a snowstorm

2.

He is _____ his shirt.

(A) ironing
(B) patching
(C) mending
(D) discarding

Part B. Sentence Completion

3. Gina is into all kinds of extreme sports these days. She's very _____.

(A) adventure
(B) adventurer
(C) adventuring
(D) adventurous

4. This event _____ place in all kinds of weather.

(A) took it
(B) was taken
(C) has taken
(D) has been taken

Extreme Ironing Player Chart

Marion Kilgaard

- Representing: Germany
- Garments ironed competitively: 7
- Burns received from iron: 3
- Most extreme ironing moment: skydiving from a plane
- Least favorite real-life ironing: pleats in skirts

Sanjay Anand

- Representing: India
- Garments ironed competitively: 8
- Burns received from iron: 1
- Most extreme ironing moment: during a bicycle race
- Least favorite real-life ironing: shirt collars

Kris Parnmore

- Representing: Canada
- Garments ironed competitively: 5
- Burns received from iron: 4
- Most extreme ironing moment: in the middle of the desert
- Least favorite real-life ironing: pockets

Tiana Ballas

- Representing: Greece
- Garments ironed competitively: 7
- Burns received from iron: 6
- Most extreme ironing moment: paragliding over a valley
- Least favorite real-life ironing: any item with buttons

5. Who most likely got burned while cycling?

(A) Marion Kilgaard
(B) Sanjay Anand
(C) Kris Parnmore
(D) Tiana Ballas

6. According to the chart, which of the following is true?

(A) An Indian competitor ironed silk pockets.
(B) An athlete from Germany ironed in a desert.
(C) A Canadian received five burns while ironing.
(D) A Greek athlete dislikes ironing button-down shirts.

Part D. General Reading Comprehension

[1] Ironing a shirt is a challenge for many people. In the competitive sport of extreme ironing, however, that challenge is taken to a different level as competitors press clothing in extreme places and conditions.

[2] There are different rules for the diverse extreme ironing competitions held around the world, but the general rules are similar. Ironers must have a full-sized ironing board, a real iron, and a piece of clothing larger than a face towel. Very importantly, the ironers need to be video-recorded so that others can see them compete.

[3] Spectators cannot typically view the competitors in action because the ironing needs to take place in extreme conditions. In the past, contestants have ironed in trees, on rooftops, on steep cliffs, on mountaintops, on ropes suspended between rocks, in icy glacier water, and in dry deserts. Extreme ironing has even happened on the ocean floor by ironers who were divers.

[4] Extreme ironers are advised to take safety precautions. However, like all extreme sports, this kind of ironing comes with some risks. For adventurous athletes who also want to complete household chores, extreme ironing might be just the right kind of competition.

7. Which paragraph is mainly about the competition's regulations?

(A) paragraph 1
(B) paragraph 2
(C) paragraph 3
(D) paragraph 4

8. How are competitors generally seen by spectators?

(A) in a stadium
(B) in a living room
(C) via photographs
(D) via video recordings

9. What location of extreme ironing is NOT mentioned?

(A) deserts
(B) surfboards
(C) glacier water
(D) mountaintops

10. Which of the following are competitors warned to remember?

(A) price
(B) safety
(C) face towels
(D) colorful clothing

Listening Practice

 Listen and write.

  MP3 HJ1-7

Extreme Ironing

Ironing a shirt is a challenge for many people. In the competitive sport of extreme

₁_____, however, that challenge is taken to a different level as competitors

₂_____ clothing in extreme places and conditions.
There are different rules for the diverse extreme ironing competitions held around the world,
but the general rules are similar. Ironers must have a full-sized ironing board, a real iron, and
a piece of clothing larger than a face towel. Very importantly, the ironers need to be video-
recorded so that others can see them compete.

Spectators cannot typically view the competitors in action because the ironing needs to take place
in extreme conditions. In the past, contestants have ironed in trees, on rooftops, on steep cliffs,

on mountaintops, on ropes ³_____ between rocks, in icy ⁴_____

water, and in dry deserts. Extreme ironing has even happened on the ocean floor by ironers who
were divers.

Extreme ironers are advised to take safety ⁵_____. However, like all extreme
sports, this kind of ironing comes with some risks. For adventurous athletes who also want

to complete household ⁶_____, extreme ironing might be just the right kind of
competition.

Word Bank

press	gracier	puress
glacier	shores	chores
precaution	suspended	precautions
ironing	ierning	suspend

 Listen. Pause. Say each sentence.

  MP3 HJ1-7G

Writing Practice

 Write the words.

1 _____

   v take wrinkles out of clothes

2 _____

   v iron

3 _____

   n a big mass of ice

4 _____

   adj hanging

5 _____

   n a way to avoid risk

6 _____

   n a task

 Write the words in each blank.

Summary

In extreme ironing competitions, competitors iron clothing in a variety of extreme

_____. The ironers need to be video-recorded for _____. The

competition is good for _____ athletes who want to take some risk while completing

_____ chores.

Word Puzzle

 Complete the word puzzle.

Across

3 a way to avoid risk

6 iron

Down

1 a big mass of ice

2 hanging

4 a task

5 take wrinkles out of clothes

Teacher's Book p.81

UNIT 8

The Heso Odori

Look at the picture. Which country does it remind you of?

The Heso Odori, or Belly Button Dance competition, was not always popular. The competition, which is part of a larger festival celebrating the belly button in Hokkaido, Japan, was started because city authorities thought the town of Furano needed its own festival for economic reasons. They chose the belly button theme based on the town's location in the middle of Hokkaido. In 1969, the first year of the dance, there were only eleven dancers. However, over time, the dance grew into a major event for the town. Half a century later, there are over 4,000 dancers and tens of thousands of locals and tourists watching them each year.

In the Heso Odori, dancers must transform their belly button into a face through decorations. They can use special costumes, props, and paint to do so. The dancers then parade through the town, dancing with humor and enthusiasm. Prizes are given in a range of categories, but the connecting theme is to have fun by celebrating the seemingly humble yet important belly button.

New Words

belly button	**authority**
n a small hole in the middle of your stomach area	*n* an official
transform	**prop**
v change completely	*n* an object used in the theater
enthusiasm	**humble**
n positive energy	*adj* modest

Part A. Picture Description

1.

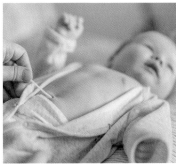

She is cleaning the baby's _____.

(A) wrists
(B) earlobe
(C) knee caps
(D) belly button

2.

These are the _____ we will need for the show.

(A) wigs
(B) props
(C) scripts
(D) costumes

Part B. Sentence Completion

3. I thought this room _____ some color, so I painted the walls.

(A) need
(B) needs
(C) needed
(D) has been needed

4. _____ spectators watch the performers every year.

(A) Hundreds
(B) Hundreds of
(C) A hundred of
(D) The hundreds

Part C. Practical Reading Comprehension

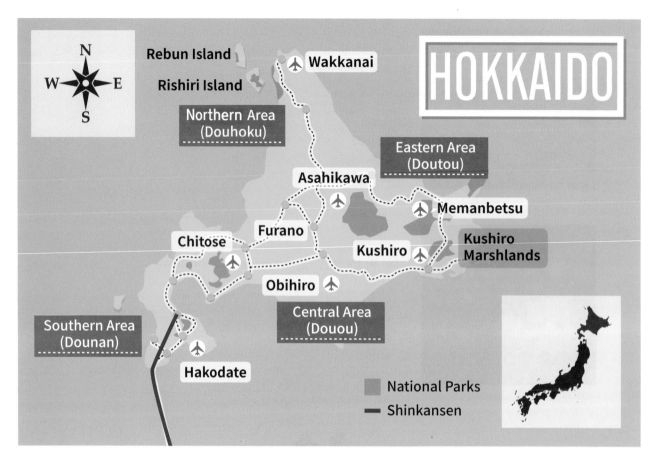

5. According to the map, which of the following is true?

   (A) Furano is in the Dounan.
   (B) Obihiro is northeast of Hakodate.
   (C) The Marshlands are in the Douou.
   (D) Wakkanai is to the west of Rebun Island.

6. Which of the following is on the map?

   (A) local delicacies
   (B) ferry information
   (C) compass directions
   (D) town populations

Part D. General Reading Comprehension

The Heso Odori, or Belly Button Dance competition, was not always popular. The competition, which is part of a larger festival celebrating the belly button in Hokkaido, Japan, was started because city authorities thought the town of Furano needed its own festival for economic reasons. They chose the belly button theme based on the town's location in the middle of Hokkaido. In 1969, the first year of the dance, there were only eleven dancers. However, over time, the dance grew into a major event for the town. Half a century later, there are over 4,000 dancers and tens of thousands of locals and tourists watching them each year.

In the Heso Odori, dancers must transform their belly button into a face through decorations. They can use special costumes, props, and paint to do so. The dancers then parade through the town, dancing with humor and enthusiasm. Prizes are given in a range of categories, but the connecting theme is to have fun by celebrating the seemingly humble yet important belly button.

7. What would be the best title for the passage?

(A) Heso Odori: An Ancient Ritual
(B) Japanese Foods and Festivals
(C) Heso Odori: Hokkaido Snow Dance
(D) Japan's Belly Button Dance Contest

8. Why did Furano choose the festival theme of belly buttons?

(A) The town is full of medical schools.
(B) The town is in the middle of Hokkaido.
(C) The town is in the shape of a belly button.
(D) The town is where Japan's oldest person lives.

9. Which of the following is true about the Heso Odori?

(A) It was started for financial purposes.
(B) In 1969, it celebrated its centennial year.
(C) Over a hundred people joined the first dance.
(D) The mayor selects 11 people to join each year.

10. Which of the following is NOT mentioned in the passage?

(A) paint
(B) props
(C) clowns
(D) costumes

Listen and write.

MP3 HJ1-8

The Heso Odori

The Heso Odori, or Belly Button Dance competition, was not always popular. The competition, which is part of a larger festival celebrating the ___1___ in Hokkaido, Japan, was started because city ___2___ thought the town of Furano needed its own festival for economic reasons. They chose the belly button theme based on the town's location in the middle of Hokkaido. In 1969, the first year of the dance, there were only eleven dancers. However, over time, the dance grew into a major event for the town. Half a century later, there are over 4,000 dancers and tens of thousands of locals and tourists watching them each year.

In the Heso Odori, dancers must ___3___ their belly button into a face through decorations. They can use special costumes, ___4___, and paint to do so. The dancers then parade through the town, dancing with humor and ___5___. Prizes are given in a range of categories, but the connecting theme is to have fun by celebrating the seemingly ___6___ yet important belly button.

Word Bank

belly button	authoritys	humble
transform	entusiasm	enthusiasm
trensform	bely buton	props
authorities	humbel	propps

Listen. Pause. Say each sentence.

MP3 HJ1-8G

Writing Practice

 Write the words.

1 _____

_n_ a small hole in the middle of your stomach area

2 _____

_n_ an official

3 _____

_v_ change completely

4 _____

_n_ an object used in the theater

5 _____

_n_ positive energy

6 _____

adj modest

 Write the words in each blank.

Summary

The Heso Odori is a competition in Hokkaido that celebrates the _____. In this event, dancers _____ their belly button into a face and use special costumes, _____, and paint. Also, _____ are given to have fun by celebrating the belly button.

Word Puzzle

 Complete the word puzzle.

Across

3 a small hole in the middle of your stomach area

6 an official

Down

1 modest

2 an object used in the theater

4 positive energy

5 change completely

El Santo: Mexico's Masked Man of Mystery

Teacher's Book p.85

In the sport of Mexican wrestling, or *lucha libre*, competitors wear masks. They only remove their masks if they lose in the ring. Rodolfo Guzmán Huerta was undoubtedly Mexico's most famous wrestler. However, to most people, his actual face was a complete mystery. That is because in 1942, he put on his mask under the wrestling name "El Santo." And because he rarely lost, he did not remove the mask.

El Santo was like a superhero. First, he became the star of a comic book series. Then, he became a movie star, playing the lead in more than fifty films. In every movie, he wore his mask. If he walked down the street, he walked in his mask. Even when he went to eat, he wore a special mask. The whole time, he kept wrestling. He competed as a wrestler until the age of 64 in 1982. For forty years, Guzmán Huerta had been El Santo, complete with his mask on at all times.

In 1984, El Santo appeared on a talk show. During his appearance, he finally took off his mask. It was a huge moment for the Mexican public and for fans of *lucha libre*. The mystery of the face of El Santo had been solved. However, ten days after removing his mask, El Santo died of a heart attack. Did he sense he was going to die? Is that why he removed his mask? It is one of the unsolved mysteries of the wrestling world. What we do know is that El Santo was not buried with his face uncovered, but wearing his famous mask.

CHAPTER 3

Competitions 3

UNIT 9

Teacher's Book p.86

Making Faces

How many different ugly faces can you make?

The Spanish city of Bilbao and the English town of Egremont share an interesting type of competition: one in which the contestants have to make the ugliest face they can. While both competitions share some similarities, they also have a few differences.

Egremont's contest is called the World Gurning Championships. "Gurning" is the act of making an ugly face on purpose. In the competition, contestants put their head through a horse collar as they make the face. The face can be similar to someone eating something very sour. Indeed, the competition may have started back in the year 1267, when a royal lord gave sour fruit to the villagers at a fair.

The Bilbao contest, on the other hand, is much more recent. It began in 1978 as part of the town's "Aste Nagusia" ("Great Week") festival. In this contest, rather than jutting out the teeth, contestants try to look as gross as possible. This often involves using their hands to pull the skin around the eyes while pushing up their nose. Whereas competitors in the World Gurning Championships tend to be adults, in Bilbao, people of all ages participate.

New Words

ugly	**make a face**
adj not attractive	*v* move your facial features into an ugly or funny expression
similarity	**sour**
n something that is the same	*adj* not sweet, not salty; like the taste of a lemon
jut out	**gross**
v extend out	*adj* disgusting

Part A. Picture Description

1.

A big rock _____ the middle of the island.

(A) runs into
(B) sinks into
(C) juts out from
(D) floats away from

2.

His face shows he ate something _____.

(A) sour
(B) sweet
(C) savory
(D) special

Part B. Sentence Completion

3. You're in a contest? What _____?

(A) that involves
(B) involves that
(C) is that involve
(D) does that involve

4. This book is similar _____ the one that I read last month.

(A) to
(B) in
(C) for
(D) around

1. **Have no teeth.**
   It makes it easier to twist your mouth into crazy positions. That's why one gurning champion had his teeth surgically removed.

2. **It helps to be British.**
   No other nationality has won!

3. **Be good-looking in general.**
   Gurning is judged by the size of the transformation you make. If you already have a naturally attractive face, the transformation to an ugly gurning expression can be very big!

5. What would be the best title for the passage?

   (A) Where to Witness Gurning
   (B) How to Win a Gurning Contest
   (C) Where to Go to Practice Gurning
   (D) How to Judge a Gurning Championship

6. According to the passage, which of the following statements is true?

   (A) A gurner must be British.
   (B) A champion's teeth were removed.
   (C) Points are given to gurners for smiling at the judges.
   (D) Points are awarded for showing attractive expressions.

Part D. General Reading Comprehension

The Spanish city of Bilbao and the English town of Egremont share an interesting type of competition: one in which the contestants have to make the ugliest face they can. While both competitions share some similarities, they also have a few differences.

Egremont's contest is called the World Gurning Championships. "Gurning" is the act of making an ugly face on purpose. In the competition, contestants put their head through a horse collar as they make the face. The face can be similar to someone eating something very sour. Indeed, the competition may have started back in the year 1267, when a royal lord gave sour fruit to the villagers at a fair.

The Bilbao contest, on the other hand, is much more recent. It began in 1978 as part of the town's "Aste Nagusia" ("Great Week") festival. In this contest, rather than jutting out the teeth, contestants try to look as gross as possible. This often involves using their hands to pull the skin around the eyes while pushing up their nose. Whereas competitors in the World Gurning Championships tend to be adults, in Bilbao, people of all ages participate.

7. Which of the following would be the best title for the passage?

(A) The Long History of Gurning
(B) How to Get Ugly in Two Competitions
(C) How to Gurn at the Aste Nagusia
(D) Why Spain Adopted an English Custom

8. What kind of face would competitors in Egremont most likely make?

(A) one like they were eating a lemon
(B) one like they were eating soft cake
(C) one like they were riding a fast horse
(D) one like they were riding a slow bicycle

9. What do competitors in the Bilbao contest do differently from those in Egremont?

(A) put a collar on a horse
(B) pull the skin on their stomach
(C) use their hands to look disgusting
(D) set their teeth out as far as possible

10. When did Bilbao's contest begin?

(A) 1267
(B) 1978
(C) when a royal lord gave villages fruit
(D) when children were banned from the festival

 Listen and write.

  MP3 HJ1-9

Making Faces

The Spanish city of Bilbao and the English town of Egremont share an interesting

type of competition: one in which the contestants have to ¹ _____ the

² _____ face they can. While both competitions share some

³ _____ , they also have a few differences.

Egremont's contest is called the World Gurning Championships. "Gurning" is the act of

making an ugly face on purpose. In the competition, contestants put their head through a

horse collar as they make the face. The face can be similar to someone eating something very

⁴ _____ . Indeed, the competition may have started back in the year 1267, when a

royal lord gave sour fruit to the villagers at a fair.

The Bilbao contest, on the other hand, is much more recent. It began in 1978 as part of the

town's "Aste Nagusia" ("Great Week") festival. In this contest, rather than ⁵ _____

out the teeth, contestants try to look as ⁶ _____ as possible. This often involves

using their hands to pull the skin around the eyes while pushing up their nose. Whereas

competitors in the World Gurning Championships tend to be adults, in Bilbao, people of all ages

participate.

Word Bank

sowr	ugliest	jutting
make	juting	similaritys
gloss	gross	sour
made	similarities	uglist

 Listen. Pause. Say each sentence.

  MP3 HJ1-9G

Writing Practice

  Write the words.

1 _____

adj not attractive

2 _____

v move your facial features into an ugly or funny expression

3 _____

n something that is the same

4 _____

adj not sweet, not salty; like the taste of a lemon

5 _____

v extend out

6 _____

adj disgusting

  Write the words in each blank.

Summary

Egremont in the UK and Bilbao in Spain _____ have contests in which _____ make the ugliest _____ they can. But there are also some _____ between each of the contests.

Word Puzzle

 Complete the word puzzle.

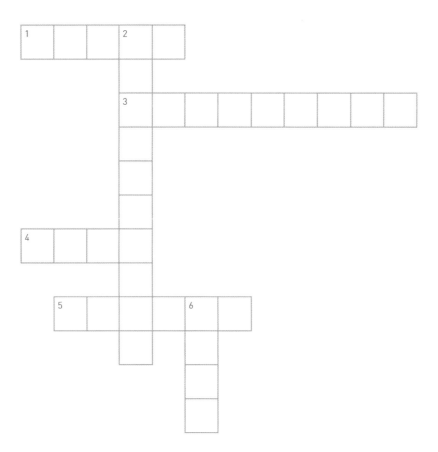

Across

1 disgusting

3 move your facial features into an ugly or funny expression

4 not sweet, not salty; like the taste of a lemon

5 extend out

Down

2 something that is the same

6 not attractive

UNIT 10

The Argungu Fishing Festival

Teacher's Book p.91

Have you ever caught a fish?

At the four-day Argungu International Fishing and Cultural Festival in northwestern Nigeria, events include a series of "kabanci," or water competitions. There are canoe races and duck catching on the Matan Fada River. But the main event on the final day is hand fishing.

During the hand fishing competition, over 5,000 fishermen and women get to the edge of the river. When they hear a gun go off, they jump into the water in search of the biggest fish. Modern fishing equipment is not permitted. Instead, the competitors use traditional nets and a gourd* made out of a dried squash.

Once the fishermen and women are in the water, drummers on canoes come out to drive the fish to shallow water with loud sounds. Fish, people, and nets are everywhere. The cash prize goes to the person who catches the largest fish.

The fishing competition and festival help maintain peace between neighboring communities, who join together in a cultural practice that also keeps the river water clear and protected. Although the festival had been stopped for years, in 2018 it was reinstated. Since 2016, the festival and its various competitions have been listed as important cultural heritage by UNESCO.

* gourd = a hard-shelled fruit, like a pumpkin

New Words

a gun goes off	drive X to
a gun makes an explosion	*v* make X go in the direction of

shallow	practice
adj not deep	*n* tradition

reinstate X	heritage
v make X happen again	*n* something of special value from previous generations

Part A. Picture Description

1.

The firework is about to _____.

(A) go off
(B) turn on
(C) stay up
(D) turn round

2.

LEFT   RIGHT

On the left, the water is relatively _____.

(A) deep
(B) sandy
(C) shallow
(D) dangerous

Part B. Sentence Completion

3. The prize will go to _____ catches the biggest fish. I hope I win this year!

(A) whoever
(B) however
(C) whenever
(D) whatsoever

4. This cultural practice _____ by UNESCO since 2016.

(A) has recognized
(B) will have recognized
(C) has been recognized
(D) will have been recognized

— **ARGUNGU, NIGERIA** ———————— **March 17, 2008**

Bello Yakub (aged 48) wrestled by hand a 65 kg fish out of the Matan Fada River at this year's Argungu Fishing Festival. The catch was the biggest of the day and netted the fisherman prizes worth four million naira (approximately US$ 34,200), including a car, fishing gear, cash, and a trip as a pilgrim to Mecca. As onlookers, including a row of local and international V.I.P.s, cheered from the banks of the river, the hour-long fishing competition ended with a row of the largest fish lined up to be weighed. The judges easily selected the gray Giwan Rua ("elephant of the water") fish as the winning catch. It did not quite beat the 2005 record of 75 kg, but it was nonetheless a very impressive haul.

5. According to the article, what is true about the winner?

   (A) He was 49 years old.
   (B) He netted a gray fish.
   (C) He set the all-time record.
   (D) He won 4,000,000 naira in cash.

6. Who is NOT mentioned in the passage?

   (A) judges
   (B) spectators
   (C) visiting family
   (D) important locals

Part D. General Reading Comprehension

At the four-day Argungu International Fishing and Cultural Festival in northwestern Nigeria, events include a series of "kabanci," or water competitions. There are canoe races and duck catching on the Matan Fada River. But the main event on the final day is hand fishing.

During the hand fishing competition, over 5,000 fishermen and women get to the edge of the river. When they hear a gun go off, they jump into the water in search of the biggest fish. Modern fishing equipment is not permitted. Instead, the competitors use traditional nets and a gourd* made out of a dried squash.

Once the fishermen and women are in the water, drummers on canoes come out to drive the fish to shallow water with loud sounds. Fish, people, and nets are everywhere. The cash prize goes to the person who catches the largest fish.

The fishing competition and festival help maintain peace between neighboring communities, who join together in a cultural practice that also keeps the river water clear and protected. Although the festival had been stopped for years, in 2018 it was reinstated. Since 2016, the festival and its various competitions have been listed as important cultural heritage by UNESCO.

* gourd = a hard-shelled fruit, like a pumpkin

7. What is the passage mainly about?

   (A) a drumming show near water
   (B) an African duck-catching contest
   (C) a Nigerian hand-fishing competition
   (D) a rowing race on a lake in Argungu

8. Which of the following is NOT mentioned?

   (A) the usual number of competitors
   (B) the place where the competition happens
   (C) the month in which the competition occurs
   (D) the equipment that is used by competitors

9. What role do the drummers play?

   (A) helping fish to jump
   (B) hitting fish with drumsticks
   (C) catching fish in large drums
   (D) chasing fish to shallow water

10. According to the passage, what is true about the festival?

   (A) It lasts three days each year.
   (B) It makes the river dirtier overall.
   (C) It was banned in 2016 by the U.N.
   (D) It has official important heritage status.

UNIT 10   The Argungu Fishing Festival

Listening Practice

 Listen and write.

  MP3 HJ1-10

The Argungu Fishing Festival

At the four-day Argungu International Fishing and Cultural Festival in northwestern Nigeria, events include a series of "kabanci," or water competitions. There are canoe races and duck catching on the Matan Fada River. But the main event on the final day is hand fishing.

During the hand fishing competition, over 5,000 fishermen and women get to the edge of the river. When they hear a gun ¹_____, they jump into the water in search of the biggest fish. Modern fishing equipment is not permitted. Instead, the competitors use traditional nets and a gourd made out of a dried squash.

Once the fishermen and women are in the water, drummers on canoes come out to ²_____ to ³_____ water with loud sounds. Fish, people, and nets are everywhere. The cash prize goes to the person who catches the largest fish.

The fishing competition and festival help maintain peace between neighboring communities, who join together in a cultural ⁴_____ that also keeps the river water clear and protected. Although the festival had been stopped for years, in 2018 it was ⁵_____ . Since 2016, the festival and its various competitions have been listed as important cultural ⁶_____ by UNESCO.

Word Bank

shalow	go off	heretige
practices	heritage	practice
drive fish	gooff	reinstate
reinstated	shallow	drive the fish

 Listen. Pause. Say each sentence.

 MP3 HJ1-10G

Writing Practice

 Write the words.

1 _____

a gun makes an explosion

2 _____ X to

v make X go in the direction of

3 _____

adj not deep

4 _____

n tradition

5 _____ X

v make X happen again

6 _____

n something of special value from previous generations

 Write the words in each blank.

Summary

During the hand fishing competition at Argungu's International Fishing and Cultural Festival in Nigeria, people _____ to catch the biggest fish using only _____ tools. The festival has been _____ as important cultural _____ by UNESCO.

Word Puzzle

 Complete the word puzzle.

Across

1 not deep

3 tradition

5 make X happen again

6 a gun makes an explosion

Down

2 something of special value from previous generations

4 make X go in the direction of

UNIT 11

Teacher's Book p.96

ClauWau

Which would you rather do, and why:
1) ride on a sled, or
2) drive a snowmobile?

Each November the Swiss winter resort of Samnaum sees a giant influx of Santas. The red-suited competitors are there for the Santa Claus World Championships, also known as ClauWau.

Over two days, 32 teams of four people per team spar in five snow-related events over six hours while dressed as Santa Claus. It might be expected that Santa Claus competitors would have to do such Santa-associated tasks as climbing down chimneys, eating milk and cookies, and delivering presents. However, at ClauWau, contestants must show off their physical endurance and agility by doing things like racing on sleds, climbing up (not down) a chimney, riding on mechanical reindeer without falling off, and driving snowmobiles while catching gifts in a fishing net.

One key purpose of ClauWau is likely just to draw visitors to the ski resort; however, both competing in and watching the events are free of charge. For any travelers heading to Switzerland, ClauWau can be a festive way to celebrate the winter season before heading down the ski hill.

New Words

influx of X	spar
n an arrival of many X	*v* compete
show off	agility
v show your abilities proudly	*n* ability to move quickly and easily
sled	reindeer
n a vehicle that can move on snow or ice	*n* a type of deer with large antlers

Part A. Picture Description

1.

It's a _____ in a scarf!

(A) bear
(B) husky
(C) penguin
(D) reindeer

2.

Rex the dog is _____ his agility.

(A) looking up
(B) hiding away
(C) showing off
(D) tearing down

Part B. Sentence Completion

3. How long can you stand on a skateboard without _____ off?

(A) fall
(B) falling
(C) you fall
(D) being fallen

4. _____ that we would need to bring our own pens to class, but why do we need our own computers?

(A) Might it be expected
(B) It might be expected
(C) There might be expected
(D) Might there be expectation

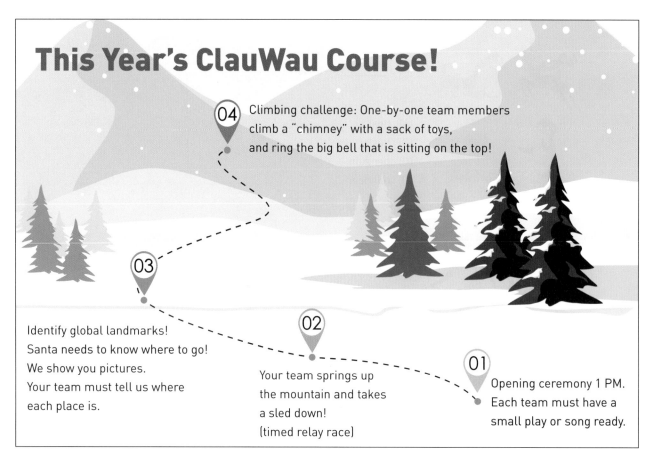

This Year's ClauWau Course!

04 Climbing challenge: One-by-one team members climb a "chimney" with a sack of toys, and ring the big bell that is sitting on the top!

03 Identify global landmarks! Santa needs to know where to go! We show you pictures. Your team must tell us where each place is.

02 Your team springs up the mountain and takes a sled down! (timed relay race)

01 Opening ceremony 1 PM. Each team must have a small play or song ready.

5. What do competitors need to prepare?

(A) a GPS device
(B) a sack of toys
(C) a formal speech
(D) a short performance

6. What can be inferred about the climbing challenge?

(A) The chimney is fake.
(B) It takes place before 1 PM.
(C) Competitors must carry a bell.
(D) Team members compete all at once.

Part D. General Reading Comprehension

Each November the Swiss winter resort of Samnaum sees a giant influx of Santas. The red-suited competitors are there for the Santa Claus World Championships, also known as ClauWau.

Over two days, 32 teams of four people per team spar in five snow-related events over six hours while dressed as Santa Claus. It might be expected that Santa Claus competitors would have to do such Santa-associated tasks as climbing down chimneys, eating milk and cookies, and delivering presents. However, at ClauWau, contestants must show off their physical endurance and agility by doing things like racing on sleds, climbing up (not down) a chimney, riding on mechanical reindeer without falling off, and driving snowmobiles while catching gifts in a fishing net.

One key purpose of ClauWau is likely just to draw visitors to the ski resort; however, both competing in and watching the events are free of charge. For any travelers heading to Switzerland, ClauWau can be a festive way to celebrate the winter season before heading down the ski hill.

7. What is the main topic of this passage?

(A) a gift giving charity
(B) a holiday sporting event
(C) a snow sculpture display
(D) a Santa skiing competition

8. How many people can compete in ClauWau each year?

(A) 4
(B) 6
(C) 32
(D) 128

9. Where is ClauWau held?

(A) Sweden
(B) Switzerland
(C) the North Pole
(D) the Netherlands

10. Which is NOT an event held during the ClauWau?

(A) catching presents
(B) climbing up chimneys
(C) riding a fake reindeer
(D) eating milk and cookies

Listen and write.

MP3 HJ1-11

ClauWau

Each November the Swiss winter resort of Samnaum sees a giant **¹_____** of Santas. The red-suited competitors are there for the Santa Claus World Championships, also known as ClauWau.

Over two days, 32 teams of four people per team **²_____** in five snow-related events over six hours while dressed as Santa Claus. It might be expected that Santa Claus competitors would have to do such Santa-associated tasks as climbing down chimneys, eating milk and cookies, and delivering presents. However, at ClauWau, contestants must **³_____** their physical endurance and **⁴_____** by doing things like racing on **⁵_____**, climbing up (not down) a chimney, riding on mechanical **⁶_____** without falling off, and driving snowmobiles while catching gifts in a fishing net.

One key purpose of ClauWau is likely just to draw visitors to the ski resort; however, both competing in and watching the events are free of charge. For any travelers heading to Switzerland, ClauWau can be a festive way to celebrate the winter season before heading down the ski hill.

Word Bank

show of	influxes	shreds
show off	agilitie	raindeer
influx	agility	reindeer
spare	spar	sleds

Listen. Pause. Say each sentence.

MP3 HJ1-11G

Writing Practice

  Write the words.

1 _____ X

   n an arrival of many X

2 _____

   v compete

3 _____

   v show your abilities proudly

4 _____

   n ability to move quickly and easily

5 _____

   n a vehicle that can move on snow or ice

6 _____

   n a type of deer with large antlers

  Write the words in each blank.

Summary

Every November, competitors _____ as Santa Claus _____ their physical _____ in the Santa Claus World Championships, or ClauWau, at a winter _____ in Switzerland.

Word Puzzle

 Complete the word puzzle.

Across

2 show your abilities proudly

3 a type of deer with large antlers

5 ability to move quickly and easily

Down

1 compete

2 a vehicle that can move on snow or ice

4 an arrival of many X

Teacher's Book
p.101

UNIT 12

Competitive Chili Eating

What's the spiciest thing you've ever eaten?

UNIT 12 Competitive Chili Eating

Beware the Bhut Jolokia, or as it is also known, the ghost pepper. This extremely hot chili pepper, one of the hottest in the world, must be handled with great care. In fact, it is so hot that the tribal ancestors of the Naga people would use cooked ghost peppers to clean flesh off the skulls of beheaded enemies. The ghost pepper's spiciness level has been measured at up to 1,500,000 Scoville heat units (SHU). In comparison, Korea's Cheongyang chili pepper has an intensity of around 10,000 SHU. Yet each year in Nagaland, India, competitors line up to see who can eat the most of this fiery delicacy.

The competition typically features local Naga people and a few international contestants. Gloved attendants hand the ghost peppers to the contestants on plates, and then wait on the side with powdered milk, considered a way to reduce the effects of the chili's heat. The time limit is 20 seconds, and usually the winner eats 5 or 6 peppers within that time. Winners walk away with glory, a cash prize of 20,000 rupees (278 USD), and a blazing hot feeling in their mouth.

New Words

beware	ancestor
v be careful of	*n* a person from whom you are descended

flesh	intensity
n the soft stuff under skin	*n* strength

delicacy	glory
n a special, sometimes expensive food from a certain region	*n* honor and fame

Part A. Picture Description

1.

The dosa is a _____ of Southern India.

(A) bloom
(B) market
(C) vehicle
(D) delicacy

2.

Today, the red team gets the _____!

(A) boot
(B) glory
(C) sadness
(D) disappointment

Part B. Sentence Completion

3. _____ love spicy food, I'm not eating that pepper!

(A) I although may
(B) Although may I
(C) As much as I may
(D) As much as may I

4. This is the Barry Diamond, _____ one of the most valuable diamonds of all time.

(A) considered
(B) which considered
(C) which it is considered
(D) which considered to be

Pepper Comparison

Name	Region(s) Commonly Grown	Scoville Heat Units (SHU)
Carolina Reaper	Carolina, USA	2,200,000
Trinidad Moruga Scorpion	Moruga, Trinidad and Tobago	2,009,000
Ghost Pepper	India	800,000 - 1,500,000
Cayenne	India; East Africa; Mexico; USA	30,000 - 50,000
Jalapeño Pepper	USA; Mexico	2,500 - 8,000
Bell Pepper	Various regions. Native to Mexico, Central America, and South America	0

5. Which specific region is NOT mentioned in the chart?

(A) East Africa
(B) West Africa
(C) North America
(D) Central America

6. According to the chart, what is NOT true?

(A) The jalapeño pepper is much less spicy than cayenne pepper.
(B) The hottest ghost pepper is just as hot as the Carolina Reaper.
(C) The pepper from Moruga packs more heat than both Indian ones.
(D) The Carolina Reaper is not as hot as the Trinidad Moruga Scorpion.

Part D. General Reading Comprehension

Beware the Bhut Jolokia, or as it is also known, the ghost pepper. This extremely hot chili pepper, one of the hottest in the world, must be handled with great care. In fact, it is so hot that the tribal ancestors of the Naga people would use cooked ghost peppers to clean flesh off the skulls of beheaded enemies. The ghost pepper's spiciness level has been measured at up to 1,500,000 Scoville heat units (SHU). In comparison, Korea's Cheongyang chili pepper has an intensity of around 10,000 SHU. Yet each year in Nagaland, India, competitors line up to see who can eat the most of this fiery delicacy.

The competition typically features local Naga people and a few international contestants. Gloved attendants hand the ghost peppers to the contestants on plates, and then wait on the side with powdered milk, considered a way to reduce the effects of the chili's heat. The time limit is 20 seconds, and usually the winner eats 5 or 6 peppers within that time. Winners walk away with glory, a cash prize of 20,000 rupees (278 USD), and a blazing hot feeling in their mouth.

7. What would be the best title for the passage?

   (A) The History of Spice
   (B) Spicing Up Your Cooking
   (C) Could You Beat the Heat?
   (D) How Do I Deal with a Hot Head?

8. According to the passage, what can be inferred about the ghost pepper?

   (A) It is too spicy to eat.
   (B) It can burn people's skin.
   (C) It was recently discovered.
   (D) It has been grown in Korea.

9. What is NOT mentioned as something received by the winner of this competition?

   (A) glory
   (B) money
   (C) a trophy
   (D) a spicy mouth

10. According to the passage, what is used to measure a pepper's spiciness?

   (A) SHU
   (B) USD
   (C) Naga
   (D) rupees

 Listen and write.

  MP3 HJ1-12

Competitive Chili Eating

1 _____ the Bhut Jolokia, or as it is also known, the ghost pepper. This extremely hot chili pepper, one of the hottest in the world, must be handled with great care. In fact, it is so hot that the tribal 2 _____ of the Naga people would use cooked ghost peppers to clean 3 _____ off the skulls of beheaded enemies. The ghost pepper's spiciness level has been measured at up to 1,500,000 Scoville heat units (SHU). In comparison, Korea's Cheongyang chili pepper has an 4 _____ of around 10,000 SHU. Yet each year in Nagaland, India, competitors line up to see who can eat the most of this fiery 5 _____ .

The competition typically features local Naga people and a few international contestants. Gloved attendants hand the ghost peppers to the contestants on plates, and then wait on the side with powdered milk, considered a way to reduce the effects of the chili's heat. The time limit is 20 seconds, and usually the winner eats 5 or 6 peppers within that time. Winners walk away with 6 _____ , a cash prize of 20,000 rupees (278 USD), and a blazing hot feeling in their mouth.

Word Bank

delicasy	glory	Beware
ancestors	intensity	ancestor
fresh	Bewere	flesh
galory	delicacy	intensety

 Listen. Pause. Say each sentence.

  MP3 HJ1-12G

Writing Practice

 Write the words.

1 _____

   v be careful of

2 _____

   n a person from whom you are descended

3 _____

   n the soft stuff under skin

4 _____

   n strength

5 _____

   n a special, sometimes expensive food from a certain region

6 _____

   n honor and·fame

 Write the words in each blank.

Summary

Bhut Jolokia, also known as the ghost pepper, is one of the _____ chili peppers in the world. Yet every year in an Indian village, competitors _____ to see who can eat the most of a _____ hot _____.

 **Word Puzzle**

 Complete the word puzzle.

Across

4 a special, sometimes expensive food from a certain region

5 the soft stuff under skin

6 a person from whom you are descended

Down

1 honor and fame

2 strength

3 be careful of

The Craziest Race of the Olympics —

Teacher's Book
p.107

Many strange things have happened at the Olympic Games. However, one of the oddest events occurred during the marathon of the 1904 Summer Olympics in St. Louis, U.S.A.

The first thing that went wrong was the choice of competitors. Some of them were real marathon runners who had competed before in major events, such as the Boston Marathon. However, the majority of the runners were inexperienced in long races. One competitor even appeared in long, formal trousers, business shoes, and a hat.

Another strange thing was an experiment performed on runner Thomas Hicks. His trainers had decided not to give him water during the race. Instead, they gave him a mixture of egg whites and a powdered drug. They also gave him alcohol. Hicks got very ill, and at one point began to hallucinate.

But strangest of all was when Fred Lorz was declared the winner. At first, Lorz had been in the lead. However, fourteen kilometers into the marathon, he felt sick and decided to ride the rest of the way in a car. The organizers did not realize he had taken a car and were just about to give him a medal when someone in the crowd shouted that the winner was false. Lorz told the organizers that he accepted the gold medal as a joke. Of course, the medal was promptly taken away from him. Hicks eventually made it over the finish line to win the craziest race of the Olympics.

ANSWERS

CHAPTER 1 | Competitions 1 p.10

UNIT 1 · HJ1-1 · p.11
- ⏱ 1 (B) 2 (B) 3 (B) 4 (C) 5 (A) 6 (D) 7 (C) 8 (B) 9 (A) 10 (C)
- 🎧 1 peculiar 2 come to be 3 came up with 4 clever 5 contestants 6 backfired
- ✏️ 1 contestant 2 peculiar 3 come to be 4 come up with 5 clever 6 backfire
- 📄 first, stopped, peculiar, popular
- 🧩 → 4 backfire 6 peculiar ↓ 1 come up with 2 come to be 3 contestant 5 clever

UNIT 2 · HJ1-2 · p.19
- ⏱ 1 (A) 2 (D) 3 (C) 4 (C) 5 (D) 6 (C) 7 (A) 8 (D) 9 (B) 10 (B)
- 🎧 1 mental 2 Dutch 3 alternating 4 categories 5 certified 6 exhausting
- ✏️ 1 mental 2 Dutch 3 alternating 4 category 5 certified 6 exhausting
- 📄 mental, combined, worldwide, certified
- 🧩 → 2 Dutch 6 alternating ↓ 1 exhausting 3 certified 4 mental 5 category

UNIT 3 · HJ1-3 · p.27
- ⏱ 1 (D) 2 (C) 3 (C) 4 (A) 5 (D) 6 (B) 7 (B) 8 (D) 9 (C) 10 (C)
- 🎧 1 matter 2 mastered 3 memorized 4 shuffled 5 keep track of 6 countless
- ✏️ 1 memorize 2 in a matter of minutes 3 master 4 shuffled 5 keep track of 6 countless
- 📄 Competitors, mastered, memorization, keep track of
- 🧩 → 2 in a matter of minutes 4 memorize 5 shuffled ↓ 1 keep track of 3 countless 4 master

UNIT 4 · HJ1-4 · p.35
- ⏱ 1 (D) 2 (A) 3 (C) 4 (D) 5 (B) 6 (A) 7 (C) 8 (A) 9 (C) 10 (C)
- 🎧 1 puns 2 jokes 3 crown 4 word play 5 complicated 6 judges
- ✏️ 1 pun 2 joke 3 crown 4 word play 5 complicated 6 judge
- 📄 statements, humor, clever, crown
- 🧩 → 2 word play 5 crown 6 judge ↓ 1 complicated 3 pun 4 joke

CHAPTER 2 | Competitions 2 p.44

UNIT 5 · HJ1-5 · p.45
- ⏱ 1 (C) 2 (C) 3 (C) 4 (C) 5 (C) 6 (C) 7 (B) 8 (D) 9 (C) 10 (C)
- 🎧 1 pretending 2 invisible 3 acoustic 4 miming 5 taken on 6 promote
- ✏️ 1 pretend 2 invisible 3 acoustic 4 mime 5 take on 6 promote
- 📄 annual, performance, sideshow, promote
- 🧩 → 4 pretend 5 mime ↓ 1 invisible 2 take on 3 acoustic 4 promote

UNIT 6 · HJ1-6 · p.53
- ⏱ 1 (A) 2 (C) 3 (A) 4 (B) 5 (A) 6 (C) 7 (A) 8 (D) 9 (C) 10 (A)
- 🎧 1 Televised 2 Nonetheless 3 apparent 4 infamously 5 acceptance 6 naked
- ✏️ 1 televised 2 nonetheless 3 apparent 4 infamously 5 acceptance speech 6 naked
- 📄 Infamously, mispronounced, announced, naked
- 🧩 → 2 nonetheless 5 televised 6 naked ↓ 1 infamously 3 acceptance speech 4 apparent

UNIT 7 · HJ1-7 · p.61
- ⏱ 1 (B) 2 (A) 3 (D) 4 (C) 5 (B) 6 (D) 7 (B) 8 (D) 9 (B) 10 (B)
- 🎧 1 ironing 2 press 3 suspended 4 glacier 5 precautions 6 chores
- ✏️ 1 iron 2 press 3 glacier 4 suspended 5 precaution 6 chore
- 📄 conditions, spectators, adventurous, household
- 🧩 → 3 precaution 6 press ↓ 1 glacier 2 suspended 4 chore 5 iron

UNIT 8 · HJ1-8 · p.69
- ⏱ 1 (D) 2 (B) 3 (C) 4 (B) 5 (B) 6 (C) 7 (D) 8 (B) 9 (A) 10 (C)
- 🎧 1 belly button 2 authorities 3 transform 4 props 5 enthusiasm 6 humble
- ✏️ 1 belly button 2 authority 3 transform 4 prop 5 enthusiasm 6 humble
- 📄 belly button, transform, props, prizes
- 🧩 → 3 belly button 6 authority ↓ 1 humble 2 prop 4 enthusiasm 5 transform

CHAPTER 3 | Competitions 3 p.78

UNIT 9 · HJ1-9 · p.79
- ⏱ 1 (C) 2 (A) 3 (D) 4 (A) 5 (B) 6 (B) 7 (B) 8 (A) 9 (C) 10 (B)
- 🎧 1 make 2 ugliest 3 similarities 4 sour 5 jutting 6 gross
- ✏️ 1 ugly 2 make a face 3 similarity 4 sour 5 jut out 6 gross
- 📄 both, contestants, face, differences
- 🧩 → 1 gross 3 make a face 4 sour 5 jut out ↓ 2 similarity 6 ugly

UNIT 10 · HJ1-10 · p.87
- ⏱ 1 (A) 2 (C) 3 (A) 4 (C) 5 (B) 6 (B) 7 (C) 8 (C) 9 (D) 10 (D)
- 🎧 1 go off 2 drive the fish 3 shallow 4 practice 5 reinstated 6 heritage
- ✏️ 1 a gun goes off 2 drive 3 shallow 4 practice 5 reinstate 6 heritage
- 📄 aim, traditional, recognized, heritage
- 🧩 → 1 shallow 3 practice 5 reinstate 6 a gun goes off ↓ 2 heritage 4 drive to

UNIT 11 · HJ1-11 · p.95
- ⏱ 1 (D) 2 (C) 3 (B) 4 (B) 5 (D) 6 (A) 7 (B) 8 (D) 9 (B) 10 (D)
- 🎧 1 influx 2 spar 3 show off 4 agility 5 sleds 6 reindeer
- ✏️ 1 influx of 2 spar 3 show off 4 agility 5 sled 6 reindeer
- 📄 dressed, show off, endurance, resort
- 🧩 → 2 show off 3 reindeer 5 agility ↓ 1 spar 2 sled 4 influx of

UNIT 12 · HJ1-12 · p.103
- ⏱ 1 (D) 2 (B) 3 (C) 4 (A) 5 (B) 6 (B) 7 (C) 8 (B) 9 (C) 10 (A)
- 🎧 1 Beware 2 ancestors 3 flesh 4 intensity 5 delicacy 6 glory
- ✏️ 1 beware 2 ancestor 3 flesh 4 intensity 5 delicacy 6 glory
- 📄 hottest, gather, blazing, delicacy
- 🧩 → 4 delicacy 5 flesh 6 ancestor ↓ 1 glory 2 intensity 3 beware